DREAM LATITUDE

ALIA KOBUSZKO

Dream Latitudes

faber

First published in 2026
by Faber & Faber Ltd
The Bindery, 51 Hatton Garden
London EC1N 8HN

Typeset by Hamish Ironside
Printed in the UK by Martins the Printers

A CIP record for this book is available from the British Library

ISBN 978-0-571-39544-6

Printed and bound in the UK on FSC® certified paper in line with our continuing
commitment to ethical business practices, sustainability and the environment.
For further information see faber.co.uk/environmental-policy

Our authorised representative in the EU for product safety is
Easy Access System Europe, Mustamäe tee 50, 10621 Tallinn, Estonia
gpsr.requests@easproject.com

2 4 6 8 10 9 7 5 3 1

But above all where does this certainty of being alive come from?
—CLARICE LISPECTOR, *Near to the Wild Heart*

what we will become
waits in us like an ache
—LUCILLE CLIFTON, 'birth-day'

Acknowledgements

Thank you to *Propel Magazine* and *And Other Poems* for publishing earlier versions of 'Why Did You Jump in That River?' and 'My Sadness is a Permeable Membrane', respectively.

My deepest gratitude to Lavinia Greenlaw and Hazel Thompson for their wonderful editorial guidance and encouragement.

Contents

I

II

III

I

Dream Latitudes

[DREAM IN WHICH I WATCH A FILM ABOUT A GIRL AND HER HORSE]

The pasture: green.
The sun: barely risen.

> Girl and horse stand still in field.
> Will not move.
> Will not move until
> field moves.

Horse's tail: flicks.
In this field: time unspools.
Horse's tail: flicks.

For a long time, quiet—then

> girl and horse
> stand still—
> field runs through them.

[DREAM IN WHICH I RIDE THE HORSE]

This horse is not a horse
but I ride it like one anyway: which means
to run with something else's heart
beneath me and no beating in my chest
but a bell, pealing—

                to be the sky, blue and blinding
and hammering down upon the earth.
To be the horse itself—
running long before it was
named, not knowing
the name even when it is given,
shadow, no-shadow
the name of this horse
if it had one—

                and I know this horse
is not a horse but I ride it like one anyway:
the way I ride my body—
spinning out over and over
like the earth beneath its green violence,
perpetual and yielding and circling
around itself—

                or maybe I ride my body
the way I ride this horse:
a field of windmills in its belly.
Riding through the cloak of my desires,
hands weaving into the white shock of mane
like kite-silk gliding
between fingers—

                rich and joyous and alone
as I am, riding a horse that is not a horse,
with no name and no shadow,
only a bell for a heart.

III.

[DREAM IN WHICH I AM THE HORSE]

in field   I dreamt of   the absence   of field

   which   is like asking   a body   to forget its skin:

            impossible   but necessary

            for belief   to begin

in night   beneath the thickening moon   or morning

      stretched thin   over fading starlight

   I drank deep   the full dark   full brightness

               never dawn   never dusk

   only the greenlight   of field   as it filled me

            greensick

      griefgreen   the ground   dew slick

            and my hoofbeats echoing

                              still I kept my hope

its promise of pleasure   a faint taste

                        a bell far off ringing

      or the memory of a dream   out of the field   and into

                  its absence

   where I was set loose   and I blew through the wind

            in a long whistle

      of joy   how I swung out   over earth

         running

            and running

5

IV.

[DREAM IN WHICH I AM THE FIELD]

> to be still
> to be stillness
> to contain and be contained
> to be sky-tether
> to be the keeper of trees
> to be greenness
> to be green

Why Did You Jump in That River?

That was the year we decided on giving up beauty.
No more mourning—forget the symbols and unnecessary dreaming.
It is okay to admit you're not courageous, just rest if you're tired.
The ox is sleeping beneath the blackthorn
and knows exactly when to wake—

which is not now, was not then,
the room so cold we could see our breath,
our words briefly visible.

I still picture us like this:
my hand tracing your spine,
your skin pink and translucent
beneath my touch.

That was the year we decided no new beginnings,
no more youth and terrifying magic—
just someone to change the music,
to shout:
> *Screw the doors back on their jambs!*
> *Screw the locks back on their doors!*
I am tired of seeing and being seen.

I still think about the night it happened,
on the way to some party neither of us can remember,
you drunk, though we'd agreed not to drink the wine,
and the moon was so perfect—a clean half.

I don't remember what I said,
only that I took hold of your hand.

Things I Know Not to Be True

My brother lives in a city
somewhere he forgets to call
because remembering comes at the most
inopportune moments—like say being stuck on
the tube, or right before someone daring and glamorous
wants to take him on the adventure of his life. On Sunday afternoons
we do our weekly shopping a thousand miles apart, both of us deliberating
in the middle of the aisle—where I can almost see him, hesitating between the pears
and the peaches, while I palm lemons into a blue basket. Late evening, he likes to take his gin
neat with ice, holding his lover's hand, who is one of many lovers who find him daring and
glamorous and about to change their lives with the boyish slope of his shoulders,
and a quiet smile—and maybe he would if he wasn't always stuck
on the train home, remembering he's forgotten to call,
though I don't mind that the phone never rings,
content with the knowledge that in a city
somewhere my brother lives.

My Sadness Is a Permeable Membrane

Washing my hair tonight
could have been the most pleasure I've ever had.

I wouldn't know.
I think I shampooed five times.

I can still find comfort in my thoughts
if things are only as sad as I make them—

like how I used to pretend
anyone dead was just living
in a different city.

I keep wondering what that place would be called.
I never gave it a name.

Rain, and then it came—
all at once like a terrible thing.

Reversing the Fall

This time we turn the dream upside down,
watch you float upwards—
the horse leaping back onto the bridge
from the bottom of the river.

*

This time the ladder of our palms descends, unbroken.
The chain of our hands chaining
knuckle over knuckle, lifting your body
through the air—uncontained, weightless.

*

This time we fashion the clouds—
a softness for you to fall into.
Your wings still intact, the sun dimming,
you hear us call out, the story beginning, rebeginning.

*

This time, we mend the fabric of the dreamskin.
We go where you are happening.
Tell me you can hear me when I say
in the fields of our dreams, I will find you.

The Dreamskin Dissolves

What I remember as stillness

                         was not still.

I loved the green gate, the green door,
our house in the bowl of the cliff

                         but the cliff was crumbling.

O that cliff where my brother fell—we all saw
the same ghost back then, the man who prowled the yard,

                         and the garden I ran through in terror.

I can still recall the sun, the air,
light bleaching the green ground

                         and the river rushing on, insane.

I wanted to go back there,
to find our shadows still passing

                         over low stone walls

but all is left to trees—

                         I was a child in that field.

Has It Been So Long Since You Crossed the Street Singing?

Since you woke up and strode straight out
of the room, the house,
your hair loosening, your whole body loosening into the light—
was there ever a day like that?

Wasn't that us this afternoon
crossing the street, drowsy in our bliss?

Bathed in the red kiss of traffic light,
you wonder—has it been so long since you swam
in the arms, mouth, senses of another?

Our faces in the light, held in its kiss,
arms slung loosely over shoulders,
eyes turned towards each other—
one foot tranquil on the kerb, the other on the brink.

Inside Me

Not birds.

        Yes, pain—
        clotted, given.

An absence of pearls.

        Yes, absence.

Not music.

        No great beauty
        but perhaps enough.

The way the sky sometimes fills me
with its strength.

        The little shocks
        that propel me through the day.

To anyone else, not shocking.

Not exceptional.

Only the sun crying out
into a birdless sky.

The slow, steady passing of the hours.

Yes, darkfall.

Yes, lamplight.

A fluttering.

The feeling that something within me
is rising towards an unseen centre—

wheeling around
a great invisible spire.

[DOWN INTO THE DEPTHS TO DREAM]

I.

I surrender myself
to an earthen pit

behind me light
descends into nothing

II.

strange to enter a rupture
in the earth

stranger to enter a rupture
in the self

III.

the feeling that I am
putting on my grave

IV.

the earth is warm like a tongue

V.

dreaming   waking
dreaming   waking

it becomes a kind of breathing

VI.

what is this strange imitation   dreaming light
waking dark

VII.

the feeling that I am
burrowing into the seed
of my life

VIII.

what I create
creates me

what I dream
dreams

IX.

I would like to touch
the imagined body   I am near
just once   but it is hard

X.

in the dream I am   waking
        to a dark   I can taste
        a dark   I am dressed in
    a dark veil   weighing on my body
        without sleep   I am become
            a blackening pause
            become this dark
        dream   I sail on

XI.

in the disruption of darkness
the mind fluoresces
—a kind of photography

I can watch myself
emerge
from every aperture

there—

leading into the country
of my death

a gate a gate a gate!

Once I Was a Mad Horse

was cleaver then cleaved   was ghost   was echo of fullness

was pulsing   was longing   was heat

of bloodied mouth   was white leaking from eye   was light

but not light   was something more viscous

was viscous   thick as undertow   was body of water

then the body bathing in it   was river-silt

was mica-spangled   was stream streaming through mud

was mud   was mouthful of wet dirt   was fish-wet and slippery

was round   was egg   then halved   was yolk split on plate

was hunger   was haunting   was silent then hymn

was tree-wind   was night-howling

was blow then bruise   was fist prised open

was delicate—never precious   was wild, wild thing

was small magic   was wishbone   milktooth   windchime

was strange dream   anemone   minnow   milky heart of pearl

Nuit Calls to Geb

Holy Earth, Husband of Clay—
take these, my gifts to you:

      my spine   a river
      in the length of night

      my body   arc of bow

                    [you: string]
                    [you: arrow]

      my body   blessed O of tunnel
      open mouth of cave

                    [you: mountain]
                    [you: plain]

      my voice   morning-call

                    [you: silence]
                    [you: no answer in the night]

      I   bridge

                    [you: between]

      I   bridge

                    [you: absence]

What is left I cannot give you:

      my body   blanket of sky

                    [you: green shroud]
                    [you: blanket of sleep]

      my ribcage once—filled with birds
      my heart once—ached with shine

                    [your heart: spring-winter]
                    [your heart: perennial]

How I long for this:

    the expanse of your back
    earth-warm to my touch

                    [you: root]
                    [you: anchor]

    the well of your mouth
    from which once leapt   my dreams
    undreamt

                    [you: lacuna]
                    [you: hiatus]

    now I fill with strange visions
    in the night—within them, fires—
    in fires, singing—
    Awaken Great Slumber!

                    [you:]
                    [you:]

    no answer
    I   the watcher
    I   the waiter

                    [you:]
                    [you:]

    no voice calls
    up from the darkness,
    only the air and its movement
    or stillness—

                    [you:]
                    [you:]

I Have Called You River

river, river
you who run from me   song
sung from me   you must be born
wake up   I sing you   in your wet season
filled with possible

river, river
you who stream from me   thirst
dreamed from me   O green
rushing   I feel you move
within me   bells pealing

river, river
you who flood from me   bloom
as blood from me   come back
you must rise up   dancing
carp leaping between streams

river, river
you who cascade from me   map
made from me   O blue
sprawl   I throw armfuls of light
into the wind   I grow wild
with rain

river, river
you who run from me   dawn
swung from me   forget fear   you must break
like the falling dark   I unmoor

Everything Opens Itself to Abandon

after Keats

Spring comes and goes in gorgeous catastrophe.
See the poppies with their astonished faces blown open.
The tulips, tightly wrapped, hold on to their mystery.
I have come to be among the daffodils
and the green world they live in.
But with no bower to stand beneath
I tree, I tremble.
Love pours down. I am half shy, half wild.
My hair cloaking me. You want me transfixed,
to be your silent pearl. But I veer away, shouting.
I wheel, I whirl. I have a gift no other can see.

[You asked the voice for more existence and the voice said yes]

after Brenda Hillman

To draw a boundary around my desires I had to name them.
I was so suffused within the dream of being I believed I was the dream.

There came a consciousness I could not yet comprehend.
I did not know how to separate the shape from the meaning.
I had no self that was not the body, no body that was not the self.

When I awoke, something had shifted.
I knew when to speak or sing—
but I could no longer be in the midst.

The world had demanded of me an alteration.
The *world!* That word as if from nowhere.

II

Leaving the Kingdom

The mystery
begins like this:
  —MATT RASMUSSEN, 'Elegy in X Parts'

X

I came green into the morning
sung up through rain
the moss damp
and lichen
dancing along the tree branches

I was light-flung
I clung to the earth
in my newness
joy-spangled

soon I was tending the garden
tending the body with daily devotions
he was under me over me o
he was cherrying me

I was every animal
I drank from the stream
I wet my lip on fresh
constellations

I was drunk glittering
at all the world
my invitation

X

Once I lived in a land of magnolias.
Beauty was everywhere.
It enveloped everything
in a fine layer of wax.
Though easily disturbed
you had only to look at the
next bright thing
to find that same beauty again.
A sparrow's flight echoing through the trees.
It was difficult to know
whether this was the same bird
on a new branch
or a new bird entirely.
Thoughts didn't reach their conclusions
but spiralled quietly.
Mostly we listened
for the sound of wings
and this was enough.
Around us the magnolias unfurled, pristine.
Often, I felt that I was
on the precipice of some great
feeling—I thought one day
I would find myself looking back
across vast distances.
Though it seems all my
wild revelations
were but
small steps.
Yes, I knew pain,
but I did not know it was pain.
I called it by another name.

X

I was afraid
of my own capacity.

Longing, death, longing.

Nothing bloomed
or dropped fat from the tree.

I grew tired of gazing alone
upon the earth.

Within beauty's immensity,
I could feel the great animal
unzip my skin—unfastening my spine
vertebra by vertebra.

Before this, things had arrived perfectly,
as though they hadn't arrived at all.

No, not until desire came
did I begin to unlearn.

X

I ceased being myself
and became the shape of myself.
My hair gave off its own perfume.
My face grew clearer, more refined.
Here was the border of my body.
What was once the scent of the garden
—wild and unnameable—
was now the scent of the hibiscus trees.
The birds no longer sang in unison.
Their notes diverted.
Memory and dream were infused
as milk is infused with herbs.
I could taste the blunt blue
of every skyfield.

X

Pleasure? It was a gift
I would give again.
To love nakedness
I had first to recognise it.
In the overblown world
we were struck by the bareness of trees—
O the hours we spent
undressing fruit from trees, undressing
fruit with lips, undressing peel from pith.
We watched, beguiled,
as the sun dashed her silks
against the broadening sky.
A sweet daring creature—like me,
slowly unbuttoning her dress.

X

He possesses a mythological beauty.
His hands are immaculate and precise.

She has hands of candlelight.
Hers is a burning touch.

In his eyes live the winds
that shake the soul a little.

Her eyes are wild-cherry dark.
Her hair, adrift on the water, glimmers.

He has an enlivening touch.
His body makes mine more real.

I had many words, but no use for them
until I heard her speak.

He would not, will not, admit
it was I who named the flowers.

She is the flower.
Her petal face: a little door, opening.

He fails to understand me.
I speak plainly, he speaks in allegory.

She longs for a language—
an architecture of her own making.

He lives alone
in his mountaintop mind.

Sometimes she frightens me.
She desires beauty in all things.

He looks upon me
and feels his death coming close.

She taught me this: what I long for
I cannot bear.

I thought with his easy breath on my shoulder
I could surrender my sparkling pain.

X

I am drawing a map of distances.

        The swimmer. The sleeper. The dreamer.

Another afternoon traipsing the incomprehensible
corridors of the brain. Nothing uttered.

I stir the air and am myself stirred.

My thirst surprises, amassing in the dark.

X

Really pain is its own kind of body.
A body broken, by pain, into
smaller bodies. I am tired of
fragments. Though I love them for
their echo of what once existed, for
what is still coming into existence.
I am searching for the detail that
will illumine the whole. It was not
knowledge but death—what was
offered to me, my obliteration.

X

I had no offering for the world.
I came full-voiced, ready to receive.

What was asked of me?

I walked among all manner of visions,
the light swelling magnificent,
filling the newly-vaulted ceilings of my brain—
but the mind curls in on itself.

No, it seems to say,
dreaming, surely, dreaming.

I think back towards a nothingness
where all was unreachable.

Light can be like that, a nothingness.

There is no future self.

Each of us has our own
separate and perfect danger.

X

Beauty does not exist to punish you—a lesson I refused to learn.

It hurt me to look upon the flowers, but I did not feel regret.

I was lonely before I knew godhood was as futile as girlhood.

Though still I tried to make of myself a cathedral.

I was open to any god who would take me.

I wanted to eat the light and so I did and I could not put it out.

X

Facing again the impossible task: to be awake to every astonishment.

To say: *now, now* and *now*!

But I can't make myself new again, I can't make the world my own.

Life: another line to cross once and never again.

Still the old questions keep returning—how to explain all this happening?

Who cares in the end about the limitations of the body?

I know now I must give up my shame to live—

but how to begin the work?

Without words I've only action.

In an entire lifetime there are perhaps five true moments

we can see the full gorgeousness of being.

I want to be open to the mystery.

So I unlatch the gate of myself.

I step out wearing every touch upon my skin.

III

The Ice When It Shatters

Back then you suffered, and your gods suffered too.
Snow fell and was snow.

Who knows
how you found the strength
to meet her eyes.
Milky as they were
in the black cold rush.

Her eyes, her eyes! you cried
when they pulled you up. *Vočy*,
the word in your mouth
a black stone.

The wind coming off the mountains.
Slowly, the spirit
returning with its flood.

Somewhere on the other side of the river: death
lifts a hand, brushing away the snow.

Winterlong We Were Dreamfed

In the end we went on without our gods—the city birds singing faster and faster into the dawn. We were green then and felt it. Not quite young but new perhaps, thawing as we were into our freshness. We waited but no veil lifted. Though we sensed somewhere the usual machinery of things: curtain / hair / lips parting. The daily tides of separation we possessed no will to disturb. Only sound could reach us. The clouds drifted gauze-white, inked with stormtails. Snowflakes arrived, swords poised. Fires burned in the fields and women gathered round singing in voices of wheat. We had forgotten the name for spring, forgetting speech, which our voices failed to command. In the end it was their song, their singing, that woke us, rising into the greening light—that we might lift our faces with enough strength.

Snow on the Dead

Come grief. Come dove. Come arrival of sleep.

Come frost. Come flurry. Come burial of green.

Come glimmering. Come gleaming. Come radiant ice.

Come ghost. Come silence—

come hold a hand out to the cold, to the snow on the dead,

to the dead themselves, sleeping blanketed.

Snow on the Dead

Snow falls on everything.
Not just the grave, or ground,
but on the dead. *On* the dead.

Snow touches everything
and leaves all untouchable.

It is almost painful—
everything becoming immaculate,
the soil *un*soiled.

There is a small pleasure
in disturbing the snow—

but how to disturb a disturbance?

Snow, pushing soft-mouthed at the window,
wraps all in its *alphabet of silence*.

Including the dead, who we cannot possess.

The snow falling invisible.

Snow on the Dead

How to reach you now you have gone
to a place without borders?

I would have to go beyond
the edge of myself—

where I cannot bear to look.

How to find the shape of the mind
and then to recognise it?

How to reach beyond shape?

How to find you are not reaching back?

How to reach?

Snow on the Dead

frost	immaculate
green	forgotten
silent	shaking
shadow	running
breath	flung
glimmering	in my chest
O trees	go on
spring	frost
spring	frost
you	you
pristine	snow

Snow on the Dead

a cento

I hurl myself into my grief like a dove. All types and shapes of silent night, like water like wind over snow. The world is straight ice. I walk between miracle and confusion— the difference between silence and windlessness. There is nothing to do but sleep. There is nothing but sleep. How to exhaust the inexhaustible? The world can't stop giving. Slowly you begin to add things of your own. A house, a child, a man. My life: a little tepid pool, drying inward. But I am as real as my love and my despair. I can think of nothing the heart finds easy. In the grip of the heart pleasure or pain doesn't matter. I don't understand what I feel. I'm crying, I'm crying. It takes a long time to see, to arrive and keep arriving. I practised standing as still as I could, for as long as I could. I didn't speak, I hadn't sung, was glad the stars did not come out again, the snow stinging the air. And just like that, I was whole. I was somewhere or something else, not quite dead but freer, myself unlatched. My body trembled. I did not expect to survive.

Notes

Dream Latitudes

The line 'in field I dreamt of the absence of field' is written in reference to the opening lines of Mark Strand's poem 'Keeping Things Whole': 'in field / I am the absence / of field'.

Why Did You Jump in That River?

The lines *Screw the doors back on their jambs! / Screw the locks back on their doors!* were written in response to lines from section XXIV of Walt Whitman's 'Song of Myself': 'Unscrew the locks from the doors! / Unscrew the doors themselves from their jambs!'

[DOWN INTO THE DEPTHS TO DREAM]

A 'dreaming pit' or 'abaton' was 'a real pit, standard equipment in a pagan temple. Those who entered it to "incubate," or to sleep overnight in magical imitation of the incubatory sleep in the womb, were thought to be visited by an "incubus" or spirit who brought prophetic dreams' (Barbara G. Walker, *The Woman's Encyclopedia of Myths and Secrets*, 1983).

(You asked the voice for more existence and the voice said yes)

The title of this poem is taken from Brenda Hillman's poem 'Black Series'.

Everything Opens Itself to Abandon

The line 'the daffodils and the green world they live in' is in reference to Keats's *Endymion*: 'such are daffodils / with the green world they live in'.

Snow on the Dead

The title of this sequence of poems is taken from Ben Belitt's translation of Pablo Neruda's poem 'The Woes and the Furies'.

Snow on the Dead (ii)

The phrase *'alphabet of silence'* is a quotation from Linda Pastan's poem 'Blizzard'.

Snow on the Dead (v)

The final poem in this sequence is a cento. It is composed, with gratitude, of lines (some of which I have adapted) from the following poets, in order of first appearance: Pablo Neruda, Peter Gizzi, Federico García Lorca, Bernadette Mayer, Adunis, Jack Gilbert, Gillian Conoley, Gregory Orr, Adrienne Rich, Marie Howe, Edna St Vincent Millay, Paul Éluard, Anne Carson, Anna Swir, Marwa Helal, Carl Phillips, Olga Broumas, Linda Pastan, Leila Chatti, Sonia Sanchez and Louise Glück.